THE ANCIENT MODERN WITCH

Marion Weinstein

Live recordings of
THE ANCIENT/MODERN WITCH
are available on video tape and audio cassette

Earth Magic Productions, Inc.

Also by the Author:
Positive Magic: Occult Self-Help
Simon and Schuster, Pocket Books, New York, N.Y., 1978.
Phoenix Publishing Co., Custer, WA, 1981.
Earth Magic: A Dianic Book of Shadows
Phoenix Publishing Co., Custer, WA, 1980.
Magic for Peace:
A Non-Sectarian Guide to Working Positive Magic for Peace and Safety
Earth Magic Productions, Inc., New York, N.Y., 1991.

EARTH MAGIC PRODUCTIONS, INC.
2170 Broadway, Suite 16
New York, New York 10024

ISBN 0-9604128-4-0

Printed in the U.S.A

Acknowledgements

The following people helped transform
THE ANCIENT/MODERN WITCH from lecture to book:

- Robin Bernardi — typesetting and design
- Beryl Bernardi — transcription and Equinox/Solstice times
- Sylvia Weinstein — proofreading and creative advice
- Aelise Parkes — technical assistance
- Merlin Stone — advice and inspiration

Table of Contents

Prologue

I am hurrying through dark city streets; crowds of strange-looking people line the sidewalks to my left and right. The air is warm enough for me to take off my jacket. A crescent moon shines overhead; music plays in the background. The crowds thicken. I turn a corner, and come up against a wall of people. Their backs are toward me; the music blares louder and louder.

"Excuse me," I shout to no one in particular, to everyone in my vicinity. "I have to cross this street!" A few heads turn in my direction. They are painted in clown makeup. They turn away, as if they hadn't heard me. I tap shoulders, and push backs, New York fashion. "I've got to get through here!"

No response. They stand rooted to their spots, eyes glued ahead.

I move sideways along the wall of people, looking for an opening. There is none. They are standing shoulder tightly to shoulder. My watch tells me this is all taking entirely too long, and I'm almost late. Crowds now begin to press in on me from every direction. Policemen appear, with walkie talkies. They also ignore me. I try to turn the corner, to retrace my steps, to get back to where I started from, but so many people pushing toward me make this impossible. Through the space between shoulders and backs of heads I see a golden apparition

1

approaching the center of the empty street: huge plaster unicorns, mermaids — or rather, men dressed as mermaids — in gold lamé, waving grandly, glossy dragons, Botticelli's Venus perched atop a monstrous iridescent clamshell. A parade float. Disco music blares from hidden amplifiers.

Before this gilded extravaganza rolls into the area directly in front of me, I decide on one last desperate effort to cross the street, to wedge my way through the human wall. I choose a short woman, and boldly tap her back, talking right into her ear.

"Could you move over, please; I have to cross this street now."

She turns and regards me with undisguised annoyance. She is young, perhaps in her early 20's, and has pink and white whiskers, like a cat, painted on her dark skin. She wears a bowtie and a pale pink sequined sweater.

"You can't," she informs me with simple finality, and turns back to staring straight ahead. I realize I have to get away from here before the thickening wall of people completely closes in on me. Suddenly the entire situation seems frighteningly surreal, and I struggle not to panic. Clutching my clipboard, I look up at the clear night sky, the moon, and I do magic — rather desperately — calling on The Goddess to help me get out of the crowd, back to safety, and to my destination.

Is this a nightmare, a hallucination or a fantasy? Is this Mardi Gras in New Orleans or Carnival in Rio? No. This is Halloween in New York City — Greenwich Village, to be specific; Sixth Avenue to be more specific; three impossible blocks from the small nightclub where my lecture should be taking place any minute — to be even more specific.

2

You see, I'd never encountered the so-called "Village Parade," because although I've lived all but two years of my entire life in New York, I have always spent Halloween with friends at home, or — for the past twenty years — with my coven, and at midnight for fourteen of these years in the master control booth of WBAI radio. Never in the street, and never downtown. The parade was something I glimpsed on the evening news if I happened to be near a television set. Halloween has always been a work night for me — as it is, one way or another, for many Witches.

It's an old astrological rule: *Never plan anything having to do with communication when Mercury is retrograde.* Mercury is the planet that rules communication, and when its orbit is in a retrograde phase in relation to us on Earth, one's efforts at communication could be adversely affected. This is what I've always advised people. But I also tell them this: if you happen to have a job to do, which involves communication, and Mercury just happens to be retrograde, you shouldn't give up and go back to bed. Mercury can remain retrograde for three or four weeks; and anyway, being afraid of the planets is hardly an enlightened use of astrology. Surely not for a Witch. But Mercury was retrograde in September, 1990, when we planned the Halloween lecture, when we searched for an appropriate space to accommodate my audience, suitable for both video and audiotaping — when we came upon the charming Greenwich Village folk music nightclub, Speak Easy.

It had a wonderful sound system, just perfect for recording the lecture, because folk music records were made right on the premises. It had wonderful karma, because the greatest singers with conscience and purpose had performed their most altruistic songs right on this stage! The warm brick walls were lined with ancient pictures of Woody and Arlo Guthrie, Joan Baez and Bob Dylan, Pete Seeger and Judy Collins, as well as an endless array of sincere-eyed, guitar-wielding unknowns. Once the Village was literally crammed with folk clubs. Now only one remained, and this was it. The stage was a good size, the tables could seat 150 people, there was food and drink, and a central location — not to mention the nearly perfect acoustics. How festive for Halloween! We had rejected hotel conference rooms as too cold, classrooms as too small. Besides, I enjoy the cozy familiarity of a club atmosphere; it makes the lecture more of a performance, and I'm used to performing comedy in similar spaces. When we went to look at Speak Easy, it proved to be as charming and appropriate as its description. We were duly impressed with the in-house sound system, and our technical staff concurred. Just one nagging thought remained: I asked friends about the Village Parade. Does it come near here?

Oh, no. Three blocks away, all the way over on Sixth Avenue.
Will there be crowds?

No, of course not, they stay near the parade.

So when my cab came to a halt on Halloween night, stopped by traffic and street barricades three blocks from my destination, I wasn't concerned. I always prefer to get out and walk rather than sit stuck in traffic. *No problem*, I assured the driver. I'll just cross Sixth Avenue and then two more short blocks, and I'll be there.

Anyway, *I'm early.* I congratulated myself on how organized I was this time — thanks to so many friends helping out.

Sharon and Rob are already there to let people in the doors. Pat and Jennifer had left early with the pumpkins, the candles for the ritual, the donuts, cider, Halloween candies, apples, paper cups and decorations, the list of ticket holders — everything. Little did I know that as I left my cab, ostensibly to walk a few short blocks — Pat and Jennifer were still in their cab as they had been for the past two and a half hours, loaded with too much Halloween paraphernalia to get out and walk, clutching their beautiful Halloween outfits they would not have the time to change into, tearfully pleading with policemen — cops on horseback wearing masks! — just to be let through. *We have a lecture!*

"People are waiting for me! I have to lecture in five minutes!" Soon I too was begging policemen. Mine weren't wearing masks, nor were they on horseback — and they would have liked to be helpful, but they had a job to do, to contain the growing crowds. They advised me to crawl under their police barricades to retrace my steps. They weren't even sure where MacDougal Street was. They had been bussed in from the South Bronx and other more treacherous areas of the city, where the art of crowd and even riot control was a fundamental police skill.

Menacing young men loped past us, dressed in black leather with little antennae jiggling on their foreheads, munching pizza and frozen yogurt, pointing at the floats.

"Yo, that's a woman!"

"No, man! That's a man, man!"

A friendly policewoman advised me to crawl under another barricade. Later two police partners suggested I crawl under another, just to maneuver away from the crush. I crawled under a total of five barricades in all, each time at the suggestion of a sympathetic policeperson.

It turned out there was a place you could wait, on the corner of Sixth Avenue and somewhere else ... you couldn't see the street sign. But you could line up with about a hundred other people and wait until countless Las Vegas styled floats rolled by, until a giant officer with a gun would move the police barricade and everyone would pour into the street, laughing and yelling ... and you had to really run to keep up, and then suddenly you were on the other side of Sixth Avenue.

When I reached Speak Easy, thanking The Goddess all the way, I was forty five minutes late. There was no time to comb hair or put on makeup, or even look in a mirror. I later found out that Jennifer and Pat had also just arrived. The pumpkins and other paraphernalia were being unpacked. Some of it never was unpacked. The club was filled to capacity; many of the audience in costume. A show was in progress. The house lights were out, and Dr. Kathy Lesser, the Singing Endocrinologist (who was supposed to sing later), was up on stage with her guitar and her accompanist with his guitar, and those marvelous house acoustics were ringing with folk music once again — but this time it was Witchcraft folk music. People were clapping and singing along. A worried familiar face whispered urgently up at me, "Hurry, get up on stage and apologize for being so late."

I waited till the song was over, someone handed me a hand mike, and I climbed up on stage and thanked Kathy with all my heart. Then I looked out into that sea of smiling Halloween faces, and I realized there was nothing to apologize for! Everyone was happy and entertained. No one knew anything had gone wrong.

That's the way it is with a retrograde Mercury — anything having to do with communications might *look* like disaster; but just do magic, call on The Goddess, and everything always turns out just right.

The Lecture

I'd like to welcome you all to my Halloween event. Thank you all for being here. Welcome to the wonderful Halloween festivities.

Tonight I will be discussing Witchcraft in its most ancient and most modern forms — which are actually not that different. In ancient times, Witchcraft was relevant to daily life, and today this is still true, as we will see. By the way, you will notice a lot of electrical equipment around. Now, I could not resist taping this lecture, because a lot of my constituents couldn't be here, mainly because a lot of them live in far-flung places like England and Australia, places like that. So we will be taping audio, and taping video, because we're ancient and modern. That will be the modern part, the high-tech part. The ancient part will be the magic that we do. And Goddess knows, this planet needs magic. Now, in the old days, Witches and the regular people did magic for their villages and for their own individual lives. Now we live in a global village, so we will be doing magic for the whole Earth. And I think it's not a minute too soon, don't you agree? I want you to know that this is an incredibly magical night because it is, among other things, the Witches' New Year. So first, I'm going to explain to you everything about Halloween.

Halloween means a lot of things, but if there is one theme that Halloween is primarily about, it's about doing magic. I know you're all here because you want to do real magic, and that's what we're going to do. When I was on radio, I used to do a ritual for the city — and everybody would participate in their own homes. But I couldn't see them! So it was my dream to do a large group ritual like in the old days in the ancient villages, and tonight we're going to do it.

There's so much to tell you about Halloween. Last night on my favorite talk show, they had a professor of religion, a real "talking-head" kind of guy, explaining about Halloween. Well, darlings, you're going to get even more than he knew — more than he ever dreamed. He was explaining to them and explaining to them and explaining to them. But I'll tell you something, without wanting to sound superior: I think that if you're not a Witch you don't really know what Halloween is, if you haven't really experienced it. You know, it seemed as if he studied it from a distance. But even if you're not a Witch, you can experience it.

There are Eight Great Holidays on the Witchcraft or occult calendar. This is the ancient calendar, in the shape of a wheel. Many people think that the only round calendar was Aztec or Mayan, but that's not true. We had one in the West, we still have it. It's called the *Yule*. The Yule is from the British Isles, and it pre-dates Christianity and Judaism. Halloween is the one holiday that everybody knows about, but there are really seven others. They are all astrologically and astronomically ordained; because in the old days, as we all know from Stonehenge, those ancient folk really knew the skies. They were educated. They knew mathematics, they knew some of what we now call science. And they certainly knew when it was an Equinox and when it was a Solstice, and they also knew when it was a day right in between. Halloween is a day right in between. It's called a Cross-Quarter day.

Now, all the holidays have to do with agriculture and the harvest, because that's how people lived. You know, there was no Wall Street; there was nothing but planting, sowing, harvesting — and that was it. And, of course, there were animals. So, in those days, the harvest was the most important thing. It was absolutely sacred. Well, Halloween is the third and final harvest of the year. So, we Witches say that Halloween is a time to give thanks. Because a harvest is really saying "thank you" to The Goddess and The God, and enjoying all that you have. And on this thanks The Goddess and The God build greater harvests for us. (There's nothing wrong with wanting material goods as long as they're for the good of all, and according to free will). Every holiday was a turning point from one season into the next. Halloween is the turning point from Fall into Winter.

Winter is a scary time to some people. It's dark and cold, and this was especially true in the old days. So the people believed that this time also had a lot to do with death. We don't like death a whole lot in this culture, but in the old days death was understood much better than it is now. Our ancestors understood that death was part of a cycle, and the next thing after death was rebirth. They all believed in reincarnation. So, Halloween is the holiday of death and rebirth. Now, this is a totally amazing thing: every one of the Eight Great Holidays, every single one of them is still being celebrated today by Christians and Jews — but most people don't know it. Today's holidays have names like Easter, Christmas, and Hannukah. But if you look on the old calendar, on the Yule, on the Wheel, you will see that every modern holiday falls *within a few days* of an ancient celebration. These times are so compelling that people cannot resist them. It's as if they're in our DNA.

What's going on out there in the street, the Halloween parade in Greenwich Village, is absolutely medieval. It's unbelievable. I mean, if you stop people and ask them, "Why are you painted gold? And why are you wearing these antennae sticking out of your ears?" they will probably say they don't know, but they think they're supposed to. And you know what? They *are* supposed to.

It's an ancient thing to do, to celebrate the return of life through other dimensions, which is what reincarnation is. You know, Jung said that everything surfaces through the Collective Unconscious whether we know it or not. We're enacting meaningful mythic truths whether we know it or not. I chose to be a Witch because I wanted to know it. I wanted to make it all conscious and known, and I'm still working on it. I did a tremendous amount of research and I really worked hard, and now I can share a lot of this with you. The bottom line here is that we Witches believe in magic. Every one of these eight holidays is totally magical. This is not just a little thing, or a fantasy, reserved for Walt Disney. No, this is real. We are here to do magic. Magic at Halloween is *so* powerful. So I wanted a group of live people, just like in the old days in the ancient villages, to do the magic together, because the energy and the power that we raise here is going to enrich our own lives, transform us — and help the planet. So I really thank you for coming.

Halloween, in English, literally (because we're going back to ancient England) means "Holy Evening." Hallow E'en, right? Now, it has an ancient name: S A M H A I N. Some people pronounce it "Sam-hain" and some people pronounce it "Sowen." I pronounce it "Samhain." They left no audio tapes from the Twelfth Century.

We say at this time, on this magical evening, that *the veil is thin.* The veil is the barrier between this world and the Invisible World, the world of the spirits. Every Witch and Pagan in the old days — and now I'm talking pre-Thirteenth Century; way back — every Witch and Pagan knew that on this holiday, loved ones from the other side came and joined in the celebration and the magic. And I have no doubt that they're here tonight. A lot of people think that this is why children dress up, "trick or treat," to still re-enact this, to represent beings that came through from the other side. Not only our ancestors and people we really knew, but also other-worldly creatures who live on the other side, entities that nobody quite

15

understands exactly what they are. You know, imps and elves and beings like that. And they're here too, as far as I'm concerned.

You know, up until the Fourteenth Century, Witches had no problem in society. Witchcraft didn't have a bad name. In fact, it was wonderful to be a Witch. So, that's ancient. Around the time of the Fourteenth Century things got very heavy. It was a very bad time for Witches. And even today, the word "Pagan" is believed to mean something absolutely terrible. But all it really means, literally, is "of the country." People who lived in the country and lived the old ways were called Pagans. In my company, we call ourselves "Big City Pagans" which is kind of a contradiction. But actually, I think today you can be a big city Pagan. You can love the Earth, and be a country type, but just happen to live in a big city. And what a big city it is tonight!

Anyway, the idea of doing a ritual is to stand "Between the Worlds." That's the World of Form, which is the world we all live in — we can touch it, we can hear it. Seems like it's made out of solid matter, doesn't it? In occult terms we call it The World of Form. But now, in the New Physics, they have started telling us that our world isn't really solid, that it's just our perception. It's really atoms and molecules moving at such a rapid clip that it *seems like* it's solid matter. Well, that's another story, a more scientific lecture about perception creating reality. For our purposes here, let's just say that we Witches stand Between the Worlds: The World of Form, which seems to be solid — and The Invisible World, which we can't see, but which we know is there. And when we stand Between the Worlds — that is the place where we do the magic, the place of Power, the holiday place. That is the place of Halloween.

And now I'll explain more to you about Ancient and Modern Witchcraft, and what that means. Ancient — and we're going way back in time — was when Witchcraft and Paganism were part of daily life. Everybody lived by the seasons. Everybody lived by the crops. And everybody worshipped, not one omnipotent Deity and feared one terrible devil, like people have done in Judeo-Christian tradition, but everybody worshipped a Goddess and a God, by many names and in many ways, but essentially, one Goddess, one God. It may have seemed like a lot of them because they have a lot of different names, but these are aspects of them. If you got up close: one Goddess and one God. And I do that too. And all of us Witches do. Some Witches just worship a Goddess, and some worship a Goddess and a God — today. But in those days, as far as we know, Goddess and God — that was it.

There was no hierarchy in a religious context; everybody was considered equal in the eyes of the Deities. The way that Deity effects a culture is very subtle. It provides models and roles for the people in the culture. Now, the women's movement has recently discovered this hot news: that if a Deity is male and omnipotent, then the role model for a woman — in spiritual terms — is not so great. It's not so great for men either, because the idea of having to be omnipotent and modeling oneself after that kind of Deity, is kind of terrifying and limiting. Also, to think that all evil comes from the devil is not taking personal responsibility. Do you see what I mean by modeling? If someone believes in the devil, it's very easy to lapse into projection, and say, "Evil people are over there. I'm over here with The God." For example, Saddam Hussein recently said that *God is on his side*. Well, that's not a new or original statement. Our country said that in World War II (but then it was true, right?) Every country always says that! Because that vision of Deity — vengeful and warlike — lends itself to such a conclusion: that He's going be on your side.

But The Goddess and The God don't fight. What The Goddess and God do, is have a loving relationship. Now, think of the role models that gives you. With no sexual guilt, either. Now, this is just one of the many attributes of the Goddess/God cosmology which is based on fertility. Many parts of our culture are so restrictive, that we, as a society, are bursting away from them — such as sexual constraints, laws about accepted sexual behavior. It is immediately evident that, in ancient days, those restrictions weren't there to burst away from in the first place. That part of our culture, that kind of rigidity, that fear of doing evil if you had fun — that didn't exist! (We're talking ancient now.) This is almost impossible for us to conceive of. We're all very liberated today, but we're still all constantly liberating ourselves from patriarchal concepts. Well, picture how it must have been *before* any patriarchal concepts came along! In this culture it's almost impossible to envision such an unlimited state, but we're getting there as we approach the Aquarian Age, which we might be in already. Nobody's really sure about the exact date. Maybe it started when HAIR opened; I don't know. It did start recently, or it will start any minute, and maybe it's starting right now.

In astrology, people enjoy guessing each others' signs, meaning Sun signs: "I've had too many people guess my sign. They take twelve guesses."[1] That's an over-simplification of astrology, but we do know that the Sun over our planet Earth passes through twelve signs of the Zodiac in a year. Well, in Astrological Ages, the earth passes through the twelve signs also, but each Astrological Age takes, not one year, but two thousand years. That is a long time. We are now crossing over from one Age into another. In case you didn't know, that is what this talk about the Age of Aquarius is all about. We're leaving the Age of Pisces, which was an Age where Christianity was a dominant religion — Pisces rules Christianity — and we're entering the Age of Aquarius, which is an Age when Deity will not be that clear-cut. It is an Age of *air*, whereas Pisces was an Age of water. Another good example is: in the time of Pisces, the main kind of exploration that people had was by water — you know — boats, crossing over the oceans from one continent to another. Now exploration is done by air. We're going up into outer space, and who knows who's coming down from outer

---

[1] In POSITIVE MAGIC, I quote the comedian Robert Klein. This is his line. It was funny when I first heard it in 1974, and it still holds hilariously true today. Robert Klein, *Mind Over Matter*, Brut Records, Froben Enterprises, 1974.

space to visit us. I think we're going to have some very interesting times in the Age of Aquarius, and I hope a lot of this happens in our lifetime. Maybe we'll all be able to have our next Halloween with people from other planets. Wouldn't that be wonderful? I would be so happy, I can't even begin to tell you.

Now, as I was saying, in talking about ancient times, another thing: There was no prayer; there was magic. And what do I mean by magic? I mean transformation. But not just transformation, say, by accident or seemingly by accident; instead, *directed and controlled transformation.*. Transformation that you make happen, and that you make happen in a reasonable time frame. Because there is transformation all around us every minute, but it's happening so slowly that it's not that dramatic. When something huge happens, you know, like when peace breaks out — which happened earlier this past year when the Berlin Wall came down — I really think that a lot of that has to do with magic.

Anyway, instead of prayer there was magic. Now, prayer grows out of magic. Magic is the root of prayer. And in modern Witchcraft and occult study, we go back to magic. The primary difference between magic and prayer is: with magic, we don't ask the Deity to do it for us. Now, I'm not putting down the patriarchal monotheistic Deity. I just kid Him a lot; He's OK. But we don't ask Him for things. What we do is, we plug into the Power of the universe and we join with it. We consider ourselves linked with it to such an extent that we are able to hook into that Power, and manifest the change and the transformation that we want for ourselves.

Now, a lot of you know this. Yes, I know it too — but you know what, I keep on *re-knowing* it, on a deeper level, because it is so profound. We don't have the cultural support in this society to keep on telling us, "Yes, perception creates reality. You believe something enough and you say the right things, and you work for it in the right way, and it's going to happen. Even though it looks like a miracle — it's still going to happen." Well, there aren't a lot of people around us saying that. There are people around saying, "Worship me and I'll take care of it," or "Worship that Deity, He'll take care of it," or "I'll be the middleman for that Deity, and I'll see that He takes care of it for you." And all the complicated theological scams, with people wanting credit for the Deity's work, and money for it too! It seems today that nobody says, "You can do it for yourself if you just plug yourself in rightly." *And you're plugged in rightly anyway.* You're plugged in rightly to start with!

There are certain rules you have to follow when you do magic. Not because anybody's told you to and you're going to suffer if you don't. But just because these rules make the magic more effective; they tune you in with the rest of the universe. And these rules are just the way it all works. One of them is The Law of Cause and Effect. Now, the New Physicists are having a wonderful time disproving the sequence of Cause and Effect. In the work of magic we also know that Cause and Effect can be reversed. We know that the moment that you do the

21

magic — that's the Cause. The Effect could happen in the future, or it could happen in the past. And now there's a whole study of psychology, called Neuro-Linguistic Programming, which believes that you can change the past. Well, Witches have been working with the past for a very long time. It's really helpful to change the past. It's more wonderful to change the present though. I mean, it's not always more wonderful, but it is often more practical.

In ancient times, another thing that was very important was ritual. Now, today, there are rituals too, but some of them are unofficial and we don't know we're doing them. Like the parade out on Sixth Avenue right now. That's a ritual, but it's not organized. Then there are rituals in rites of passage, like weddings, Bar Mitzvahs and Christenings, to name a few. But in ancient times, a ritual did two things. One thing was: it celebrated, it linked you into the universal powers. The other thing it did was provide a bridge. It took you from where you were, to where you wanted to be. I believe a ritual is a bridge, and when you cross over that bridge, you get transformed. There are stages in people's lives where they need a ritual. And what happens is (and this is something that we've been discovering in my coven lately) that if there isn't a ritual already set up in the culture to answer a particular need, people will invent their own. And that, unfortunately, can be messy. One very good example of this is adolescence. It's very necessary for rituals of passage to take people from being children to being adults. And there are some provisos in this culture, but really not enough. So instead, there are teenage gangs and fraternity hazings, you know. Actual rituals based on the needs of the society would be helpful, because, I think, there would be a lot less problems, and people would feel a lot less lost. So, that's the modern part: We need ritual, and Witchcraft can provide this. Another thing that was very important in ancient times, which people are starting to catch on to now, is the link with Nature. And this is not just an idea: "Wouldn't it be nice if there were no more endangered species, wouldn't it be nice if they didn't chop down every tree on the planet." It's not like that. It's that we *really are linked* to this planet. If you looked from a distance, you wouldn't see that the people on the planet were *separate* from the planet. No, we're *part of* the planet. And we are as much a part of the planet as a stone or a blade of grass — we're just part of it. It's one thing to *say* we're part of it, and it's another thing to *know* and to *feel* we're part of it. That's a source of power too, and letting go of that awareness is a feeling of a loss of power. I believe, and many Witches do too, that the main reason that there seems to be so much destruction going on in this culture, is that people feel lack of power. And so they're constantly trying to "nuclear" themselves into more power. But I really believe that if they plugged into who they really are, *that would be enough.*

This is ancient: In ancient times everybody felt part of the process of life on this planet, and in the universe. There were still mysteries in ancient times. People were afraid, and that's where the Witches came in. A word about

23

Witchcraft: Everybody thinks that their religion is the best. Did you ever watch Evangelists on television? There aren't as many of those shows lately, but if you have cable, there still are a few. And if you ever watch them, they're often saying they're the best; in fact, not only the best, but they're the *only*. So everybody thinks their religion is the best, and I don't want to come across sounding like that. But I really think that what's so truly deep about Witchcraft is this reverence for Nature, this wonderful feeling of being connected, and knowing that we are all linked — that we really are all part of each other. So when we do our rituals, we feel we really are joined. And we're not just joined; we're *joined*. Also, in ancient times, the word Witch was pronounced "wicca" and it meant "wise." As I said, everybody thinks that their religion is the best, but I think we really were acknowledged as being wise in those days, because not too many people then could read and write. I think Witches were right up there with the literate people. Anyway, that's one of the beliefs we hold today. It's hard to check, because during the Persecutions the Witches' books were burned. So a lot of the information about Witchcraft which comes to us today is so prejudiced and crazy, because it comes from the Persecutions. It comes from that time when Witches were put to death for their beliefs, and their books were burned. That happened between 1300 and 1500. Alex Haley, the author of ROOTS, has said, "History is written by the oppressors." And that's certainly true about Witchcraft. Most of the popular Witchcraft information in this culture today comes from that terrible time. Actually, it stems from one book, called the MALLEUS MALEFICARUM. The printing press had just been invented — which changed everything. I work on a computer, a word processor. As a modern writer, it's almost impossible for me to conceive of this — but once everything was written by hand, and copied by hand. So if a book was a best seller, there were, maybe, three copies of it! Until the printing press came along. After that came two printed books: One was the GUTENBERG BIBLE (which was a hard cover), and then came this terrible little thing called the MALLEUS MALEFICARUM (which was a soft cover). That was a small book that an Inquisitor could put up his sleeve and consult when he was doing his terrible work, which was torture. The tragedy is that all the negative information about Witches today — all those terrible stereotypes about having to do with the devil — that all comes from these rather illiterate, very prejudiced, politically ambitious Inquisitors, led by the two who wrote the MALLEUS, Kramer and Sprenger, and the ruler who commissioned it. For far too long, there was no competition. What's happening in the Witchcraft movement today is that people are trying to put the truth out, instead of letting these terrible stereotypes exist any longer.

Now, here in New York there are, comparatively, a lot of Witches, and people are very sophisticated. Everything's very hip, so we might not realize that quite possibly there's still a lot of prejudice out there. I hate to say it, but a lot of people seem to think that Witches are still the same as

Satanists. Too many people still seem to believe that propaganda invented by the MALLEUS in the Fourteenth Century, that Witches worship the devil! Also there's a tremendous amount of sexism surrounding Witchcraft, because the persecution comes from a time when misogyny was rampant, in the Middle Ages. Accused Witches were hags and ugly people, or beautiful women who seduced men (who had nothing to do with *that*; the men were always totally innocent). These were the old stereotypes.

Now what do we have? We have new stereotypes! I don't know if you know about them, but you should. The new stereotypes, which are not actually negative, by the way, are provided by some of the people who are converting to Witchcraft right now.

When I started out in radio twenty years ago, there were a few Witches here and there, but they weren't talking about it. I was practically the only one talking about it. But there *were* Witches. There were hereditary Witches, as well as converts, but they were still pretty hidden.

Today it seems everybody's converting. But who's converting mostly? *Feminists.* So now, you see, there's a new stereotype. For example, last summer somebody called me for an interview. Periodically, somebody calls me up to interview me, as a Witch. Usually for Halloween.

Now, in the old days when they would call me to interview me, I would be very busy saying, "I do not worship the devil, I do not worship the devil, I do not worship —"

"Come on, you worship him sometimes."

"No. I don't even believe in the devil."

"Ah, come on."

"No. The devil is a patriarchal monotheistic guy. I don't know him, I don't want to know him, I don't care about him..."

"Come on!"

And that would be the whole interview!

That was the kind of interview I *used* to have. Now: *"So you're a lesbian?"* Because a lot of feminists, for fabulous reasons (and it's about time), are converting to a religion that has always, for thousands and thousands of years, worshipped a female Deity. And that is so empowering.

Of course, the secret is that it is also empowering for men. Because, first of all, there is (usually) also a male Deity included with The Goddess. And He is wonderful. He has many names. One name is Pan: Pan, who runs around the forest with little horns, cloven feet, and is *very* sexy. Another name He has is Cerrnunnos (Kernunnos) — very magical. In the old cave drawings, if any of you are very cultured and know about the cave drawings in Altamira, Spain and Lescaux, France, you might remember those caves with pictures of people wearing the horns and dancing around. Those people were worshipping Cerrnunnos. And He has other names, like Osiris. The male God was the Goddess' consort. And this is His time: Winter. He rules Winter.

And so these were the role models for people: the Goddess and The God, a very happy couple, two Deities.

Later, this was replaced by patriarchal monotheism, where there was an omnipotent God and an all-pervasive devil. The devil did not exist in Witchcraft times, because there was no way that Witches could worship a devil. It just doesn't fit in with the whole theology. *Worship* doesn't even fit in. What really fits in is "working with" and "feeling part of." *Awareness of*, and *being plugged into Nature* — ideas like that.

There are a lot of people today embodying Witchcraft concepts all over the world who don't know they're doing it. These are people who are environmentalists, these are people who are working for women's rights and children's rights — protection of children — and animal rights. These ideas could not exist in a totally patriarchal society, which makes me think that we really are crossing over into Aquarius. We may already be there. The idea of animals having rights, for example, doesn't fit in with the patriarchal concept of "dominion over." But it fits in perfectly with the concept that we are all linked, and that every being is equal.

So there are a lot of people today who are actually doing Witchcraft kinds of things, who don't call themselves Witches and don't know that they're embodying Witch-like principles. This is evidence, you could say, that regular people can enjoy all the benefits of Witchcraft today just as they did in the old days. In ancient times, remember, not everybody in the village was a Witch. Being a Witch is hard work, you know. You have to be constantly on call, you have to be constantly aware, and you have to always be doing certain magical tasks. Whereas, just to be friends with a Witch, and to use those concepts in your life, you could benefit from Witchcraft, and lead a more so-called "normal" life. I think that's happening a lot today too.

As for ritual: Where the Witches would gather, the whole village also would gather in some magical space, maybe in a stone circle outside of town. We all know about Stonehenge, but it wasn't the only one. There were many stone circles. Perhaps a nice field, a sacred grove with fabulous old ancient trees — these were places to meet and do the magic. Well, that's what we're going to do here. To gather together and do the magic.

Now, there are also a lot of places today where people gather together and perform rituals, but they don't really know why. And sometimes they don't really know how. I mean, there are certain rituals that are kind of free-form. I think that a huge example of this is a Rock 'n Roll concert, which has everything that a ritual has: Music, screaming, dancing, and energy. It has everything but an invocation of the Deity and a use of the magic. But the concerts that people are doing for Live Aid and Band Aid and Comic Relief — those kinds of concerts, as far as I'm concerned, are sacred. They may not be using the names of Deities, but they're doing the work. They're helping people. I just love it! To me, public ritual is just the greatest. In churches and synagogues, people have mostly become very passive; and they're led in prayer by a middleman. Today, now, you can have a middle-woman (but not too many, really) leading people along. And people are kind of passive about doing what the middleman says. But in ritual, everybody does it, everybody's in it, everybody's accomplishing it — and The Goddess and The God are working for and through everybody.

When we actually do the ritual, which will be pretty soon, I would like you all to start thinking of a wish that you really want to come true. Because in this ritual you should have something that is just for you. We're going to work for the planet; we're going to work for our loved ones, but we're also going to work for ourselves. You see, in Witchcraft, everyone's equal. There's no higher-or-lower-than, there's no better-or-worse-than. Everybody is equal, and everybody has the right to have their wish come true. So I want you to start thinking about a wish, no matter how outlandish it may seem. And when you think of your wish, think this,"*For the good of all, according to free will.*" This is very important! I'm going to say it; it would be good if you said it — but it's better if you understand it: "FOR THE GOOD OF ALL, ACCORDING TO FREE WILL." This is what a lot of people don't understand about magic, and this is why all that bad press about Witches doing harm and cursing people, is not even possible. It is just not possible, because here's how magic works: You know we work with *both* worlds. We stand Between the Worlds, and we work with both worlds — this place, the visible, the tactile world, the material world — and the invisible world. We call them

30

The World of Form, and The Invisible Realm. So, as we stand Between The Worlds, tonight we do the magic in this world, here we're in Speak Easy, in the World of Form. We do the magic here. Then, it goes out into the Invisible Realm. Out into the Invisible, into that Realm which is, you know, where everything happens. And the magic happens *threefold*. There's only one law in Witchcraft, and that's called The Threefold Law, which means *everything you do comes back to you three times* — in magic and in life. And this is also how magic works. One, you do the magic in this world; two, it goes out into the other world; three, it comes back into this world—and when it comes back here, it manifests. It comes back as a miracle. It comes back as "the real thing."

Now, back to modern stereotypes: Remember I told you that this woman called me up to interview me? She said, "Which kind of Witch are you? Are you Dianic or are you a Wiccan?" And I said, "Well, they both mean Witch." She said, "No, no. You have to be one or the other." And that's when I knew there are modern stereotypes! Here's a person, a non-Witch newspaper reporter, calling me up, interviewing me, and telling me I have to be one or the other type of Witch. Dianic means feminist today — sometimes. It doesn't *always* mean feminist. It could also mean worshipping the Goddess Diana. And Wiccan — I guess she meant it's OK for men? I don't know what she meant! But anyway, there are a lot of people who just can't be categorized. Some of them are left over hippies; they're running around with drums and headbands and flutes and tambourines, and *they're* Witches. They're on their communes...Listen, they're my best friends, so let's not make fun of *any* of them. They're all my friends, including the ex-hippies, the Dianics, and a lot of the others. And they're wonderful people. It takes great courage to come out and say you're a Witch. For example, did any of you hear this? I heard that in the WALL STREET JOURNAL a day or two ago, they said that the Fundamentalists — I'm not putting down Fundamentalists; I know a few and they're very sincere — But there are some Fundamentalists who are doing an exorcism of the city of San Francisco. Does anybody know about this? This is not a joke. This is a serious, true thing. Tonight, on Halloween! These are the people who hated the Communists. Now there are no Communists left to hate, so they don't know what to do. Communists are all eating MacDonald's hamburgers, so we can't be afraid of them any more. They're not scary. So who are we going to be afraid of? The Witches, the homosexuals, and the lesbians — that's San Francisco right there! This is not funny. My friends were worried. They said, "Oh, you better be very serious tonight, because you never know..." They're exorcising San Francisco. They *think* they are — because who invented exorcisms anyway? Come on.

I've said that in ancient times, these holidays were celebrated, and they were very powerful and meaningful — if you happened to be a *farmer.* Now, how could they be meaningful to us today? How many of us are growing corn in our back yard? It so happens, I am. But it's not a lot; it's not enough to feed my family. I don't think the ancients would be impressed. The point is, today, how many of us are farmers? How many of us are shepherds? We're just not anymore. We're Big City people.

But the holidays are still true. Here is how we can benefit from them: Every time a holiday comes around, it's laden with meaning that has to do with *the turning of the seasons.* And no matter where you live, whether you have air conditioning, steam heat, whatever — you are still influenced by the seasons. You're influenced physically as well as psychologically. And psychologically is very important. So, each time — *mark the holiday!* Stop in your tracks and mark the holiday, celebrate the magic of it! This is still a fabulous thing to do. Because not all of us grow our own corn and wheat, but we all have *crops* in our lives. What are our crops? Our projects, our families, our children, our relationships — these are crops. And they're just as important to us as, in the old days, people felt about their wheat and their corn. And, of course, there are also real farmers today. For all the troubles they may be having, they still, I think, could benefit by marking these holidays. So, it's wonderful to stop and think: What is this holiday about? Is it a planting holiday or is it a harvest holiday? If it's a planting holiday, it's a very good time for starting something, such as, starting a project or a relationship, for nurturing and nourishing something that's going to grow, for having a baby. Those holidays are in the Spring and the Summer. And if it's a harvest holiday, it's a fabulous time to give thanks and to plan for what you are going to do next, what you want next. These are, of course, in the Fall. About harvests we say: these particular Deities, The Goddess and The God — they are so loving, our vision of them is so loving, their manifestation is so loving — they want us to be happy. They don't want to punish us and smite us. They really *want* us to be happy. So when we stop and really enjoy something we have, and give thanks for it, they're going to give us more. So that's one reason a harvest holiday is so important. When we work on this holiday, Halloween, this harvest, the third and final harvest of the year, we will give thanks as part of our ritual. And it will be on this thanks that the future will be built. So re-translating the holidays is a very wonderful way of up-dating what is ancient, of modernizing ancient beliefs.

I also want to say that the Ancient/Modern concept has another meaning. When you do magic, remember I said that it works Threefold. You do it here, it goes out there, it comes back here, where it manifests — but also it works in an interesting space and time continuum. It happens in *All Time*. It also happens in *All Space*. We say "Between the Worlds," but it's really in All Space. No space is left out of this particular process: Also, magic works in All Time. All Time is *NOW*. Can you believe that, can you deal with that, can you understand that? All Time is right now; past, present, and future is right now. *This is it*! So, Ancient/Modern also means a specific vision of Time and Space.

I want to say a further word about magic. I think one

34

of the reasons the Pagans and the Witches have been so persecuted in the past has to do with the effective practice of magic. But I'll say something first about The Goddess. This concept is, of course, very threatening to a male-dominated society. Now, I will really leave the details about this to my colleagues who are primarily feminist Witches. Yes, I am a feminist and a Witch, but this is not my sole identity. I'm a lot of different things. We have men in my coven. Do you know what a coven is? It's a group of Witches who get together and do magic together, a small group. Then when larger groups get together, that includes several covens, which is what this would be tonight, if we were technical.

So, of course, the concept of a female Deity has always seemed very threatening to a patriarchal social structure. It's scary. I was once in a cab, riding along, and the cab driver said to me, "Well, I'm talking to The Man Upstairs, I'm talking to The Man Upstairs..." And I said, "What about The Woman Upstairs?" And he almost went into a pole. *"What ?"* It had never occurred to him. It seems it's still such a threatening concept, especially to a very religious person. *Who's She? No. no, not possible. God created everything.* I don't want to get into that here, mainly because of time. I want to talk more about generic magic right now.

You know I am a Goddess worshipper, and I've said that She goes by many names: Diana, Hecate, Selene, Isis, Cerridwen... She has so many names, but they are all one Goddess. This huge Goddess movement is happening today. You may all be in it! I know a lot of you are. But there may be people who don't know about it, who should know it's really coming. Now, interestingly enough, articles are published, like recently, in NEW YORK MAGAZINE, and they put it down. They don't say, "Let's burn them, let's kill them." Goddess forbid — they don't say that anymore. (You know, that's what they used to do.) But they say now, "Ha, ha, ha, ha, ha, so *trivial.*" Well, *that's because they feel threatened.* I haven't seen an article at all in a major media.publication that didn't start out trying to trivialize our religion.[2] "Ha, ha, these women are worshipping The Goddess, and they're wearing charm bracelets in the shape of their uteruses; ha, ha, ha, isn't that funny?" Well, it's not funny, it's incredibly empowering, and it's certainly not trivial. It's happening in such a huge way. I've written a song with my dear friend Robin Bernardi, which we'll sing later, and it's not a hymn — it's a *hermn* .

(laughter)

No, it really is a hermn, I'm not kidding! Listen, there is tremendous, tremendous sexism in language. Now, I'm also not the main expert on that. Merlin Stone and Barbara Walker, and several other women are into that, doing brilliant work. If you stop and think about language, starting from MANkind all the way to HIStory, you know, it's very weird. And every time you give power to

---

[2] Since this lecture, both TIME MAGAZINE and THE NEW YORK TIMES have printed non-insulting reports of the Goddess Movement, so we can assume the situation is improving. I predict things will definitely get better.

the word "man," it's enforcing something — an imbalance.

Now, what I said earlier, about persecution because of the effective use of magic: Perhaps even more threatening than the concept of Female Deity is the concept that *anyone can make a miracle*, which is a basic principle of Positive Magic. You simply don't need any assistance. You just have to follow a few common sense rules which feel good because they'll make it happen rightly — and help everyone in the process — and you'll make your own miracle. You don't have to grovel, or bow down, or bend you knee, or bow your head or do anything demeaning. You don't have to feel lower than, you don't have to feel worse than, smaller than, younger than, stupider than — anything like that — or *less holy than!* Everybody is holy enough to make their own miracle. That is the incredible secret. But it's not a secret anymore. So I wrote my books which explain this. Also, other people have written some fine books on these subjects.

A lot of the principles are common sense, if you just stop and think about it. I've said that we are all microcosms of The Goddess and The God, that we are all linked, that we are all part of this planet. The Power that makes everything else happen makes us happen — and simply by being microcosms, *we can make things happen.* We just do it "according to free will and for the good of all," and that's the secret. So now I think I'm going to answer some questions. Would you all like that? And then we'll do our ritual.

Q
&
A

QUESTIONS AND ANSWERS

Q: In your *Dianic Book of Shadows*, I don't understand the concept of "Shadows."

A: OK. What does "Shadows" mean? In the 1300's a terrible time started, called The Burning Time, which lasted three hundred years, give or take. It was a terrifying time of mass persecutions. Well, up until that time, remember I said Witches were called "The Craft Of The Wise;" that's what Witchcraft was called in the Celtic lands. Witches were literate, presumably. Who can actually prove any of this? But this is what we believe, and I personally think it's true. Witches were literate, and every Witch kept a little book which was called a Book of Shadows. That's the traditional name for a Witch's personal book. It's like a diary, a menu, a recipe book, a spell book, a scientific journal, everything all in one. It was called a Book of Shadows. EARTH MAGIC is my Book of Shadows. My beliefs are in that book. The name "Book of Shadows" comes from Old English, because I guess the shadow realm was Between the Worlds.

Q: Are you a hereditary Witch?

A: No. I wish I were a hereditary Witch. I guess I qualify as "Reconstructionist."

Q: How did you become a Witch?

39

A: I did a tremendous amount of research. But I really think that I am reincarnated from being a Witch before, because my earliest memories are of being a Witch, and believe me, there was nothing like that going on in my family! I was dressing my dolls as Witches, I was celebrating Halloween.   I guess I had memories when I was a little girl.

Q: I would be curious if you could say something more about changing the past.

A: Well, the Neuro-Linguistic people change the past by changing the emphasis on memories. In that form of psychology, you change your past by choosing different memories to be the your dominant memories to influence your psychological state. Because there are multiple memories out there. That's one way.

Another example, one that I think is really impressive, involves the Native American Peoples. They're not even called Indians anymore.   They changed the past for us. Now, their past: When we were kids in school, what we learned about, and saw in the movies, was about Indians being bloodthirsty savages. In the early westerns, they were really the villains, they were the bad guys, they were scalping people. They were shown as just savage, terrible people — which justified the way white men treated them. They were only to be killed and burned, hurt and genocided.   Now, that's all changed.   Why? because *they've changed their past.* They've made their reality

40

become our reality. And I'm not saying they did this in any contrived way. They did this out of their sense of truth. We imposed one past on them; they replaced it with another. And now that past is our past too, because it shows the white people of those times in a more negative and complex light. This kind of change only works with the truth, by the way.

Another good example is when we do healing work — which is not instead of medicine. It usually works along with medical techniques, but it influences them tremendously. There are many examples in healing work where essentially, a doctor says, "Whoops, I had the wrong X-ray. Here's the right one; you're fine." Now, that's an over-simplification, but things like that have happened. And, you know, that's the most graphic kind of healing. "The tumor is gone. Maybe it was never there." The "maybe it was never there" part is changing the past. I'm getting shivers as I tell you this, because it's really incredible. Anything else?

Q: Do you acknowledge the connection between all religions and all ways of praying? I see them all as connected.

A: I believe all religions are connected.

Q: Right. So, is there a major difference between the truth of, let's say, India or American Indians and Wicca? It's different ways, different rituals, different names — but essentially, isn't it all really the same thing?

41

A: I think that it's the same thing at a real root truth area which is often very hard to get to. In the *manifestations*, it's very different. And it's in the manifestations where a lot of the cultural power is. This is what my new Goddess book is going to be about. And this is such an interesting subject, yet I've never heard it talked about anywhere else. I'm sure people are talking about it somewhere, but I've never seen it written. It's like Marshall MacLuhan said, you know, "The medium is the message." It's not only what people say is *the teaching* that's in the religion. But what also goes into the religion is *the trappings*. And the trappings can change everything. Do you know what I mean? This is actually a whole other lecture. This is a whole other *seminar*.

In the manifestation, the difference can be profound. Perceptions of reality are different, according to how people put the trappings on each religion. The form can actually distort and change the reality. For example, the Catholic Church today is a very different church from what it was twenty or fifty years ago, and very different from what it was in New Testament times, when it wasn't even called the Catholic Church. It keeps changing. And also, the people who are in charge of it, you know, *they* change it. Lenny Bruce did a wonderful routine about the Catholic Church being like franchises. A lot of religions are like franchises! This is still true today. And each franchise does things in its own style — and each one can be very different from the root of what the religion actually

42

means. There are people who are worshipping over here and doing this thing over here, and they think that's it! Yet, other people are doing that thing over there — and they think *that's* it. And they're both in the same religion. You see what I mean? It could be distorted, changed. *To get to the core of it, is within the self.*

You know, there are even distortions of Wicca. I really hate to say it. I was on a national T.V. show, for Halloween, of course. I was on a panel of Witches, and there was one woman who said she was a Witch — and it was one of the most embarrassing moments of my life. She took a candle in the shape of a naked woman and she said, "Now we'll caress it and you'll caress it, and so-and-so will fall in love with you..." and I just wanted to leave. It felt like just the worst thing that ever happened. And the host is busy with the dry ice in the cauldron. And I'm sorry to tell you, some Witches were approving of the dry ice, "Oh yeah, that's *really* good." So unfortunately, there are distortions in Witchcraft. That was such a shock to me, I can't even tell you. I thought every Witch was hip and smart and cute. Maybe they are now. We've all got to keep on our toes, that's all I can say.

Q: What do you think of Edgar Cayce?

A: Edgar Cayce — great psychic. Fabulous, brilliant psychic. I went through a time when I studied all his books, and I was really enthusiastic about him. But he could only be psychic when he was asleep. Which is not bad, considering the times he lived in — the twenties, right? Well anyway, he was a brilliant psychic. He was absolutely curing people left and right, but he could only do it in his sleep. A devout Christian too, very sincere. I found him naive and touching. He had fabulous information on reincarnation and healing. I'm not saying I agree with everything he said, because he came from a very patriarchal foundation — which, I think, grounded him in those days. But it's good stuff. THERE IS A RIVER — very good book. And there's a whole place in Virginia Beach where people can go and study — a library, and a clinic.

Q: Does the idea of Witches traveling on brooms come from our being able to astrally project ourselves while we're sleeping?

A: This is still being explored. Personally, I would take away the sleeping part. I would just say that Witches could astrally project themselves. Now, the Inquisition people said that there were ointments that were "from the devil." And then modern social scientists are saying there were ointments, you know, that were from plants, so Witches *thought* they were flying. There's no proof. I have a theory — that they *could* fly. Here's where I go back to my other planet theory. And that's a whole other lecture! But I do think flying was possible. Anybody else?

Q: I was wondering where the traditional costume,

the hat and black robes come from.

A: The Witches' costume — well, that's a medieval costume. The Witches weren't the only ones who wore pointed hats. Here's what we know today: They wore black because, during the Persecutions, Witches traveled in the dark to their meetings. It was very dangerous to go to a Witchcraft meeting, but you had to go on the holidays; you couldn't not mark the holiday. So they would wear black to be lost in the shadows. As for the hat, there are theories about those hats. First of all, if you look at pictures from the Middle Ages, women all wore hats like that. They didn't all have the brim. Some did, but they all had the pointy top. Now, that, supposedly, also, is a *Cone of Power*. When you do Witchcraft magic there's a ritual we do called "raising the Cone of Power"[3] and the hat supposedly symbolizes that. That's one thing. And now we have theories about when you sit under a pyramid — that New Age stuff which is really "Old Age" stuff. You know, you put a pyramid on your head to help your aura, your power. It's not that different. The hat can be a power point, you know. I think it's a combination of all those things, where that hat comes from. I love that hat.

Q: Unfortunately, we're all aware of the people who try to equate Witchcraft and Satanism. Do you feel that there is a threat, that there is a certain amount of

---

[3] Instructions for Raising The Cone of Power may be found in EARTH MAGIC, pp. 28-29.

wariness to be had?

A: Yes, there still might be people — for example, that Senator, Jesse Helms — who say it all in one breath, one word— "Witchcraftandsatanism." And, of course, Satanism just has nothing to do with us. It's so totally remote. I can't even think of a suitable analogy, it's so remote. But is it a threat? Well, last night my friend who told me the story about the Fundamentalists exorcising San Francisco... supposedly they're exorcising Witches too... My friend said, "Be very careful tonight." He was worried because he had seen this in the WALL STREET JOURNAL. He said, "Be very careful, be very serious." He felt a threat, but do I? I'll say this: I think it's very important to be *aware* of any kind of threat, because I have a tendency to not see danger enough. I think it's very important to be aware of it, without being afraid of it. Be aware of it, put up your protection and don't be afraid of it. It's really critical for us to spread the word and to spread the truth that we are different from Satanism. Satanism was invented by medieval Christianity as a political thing, invented not by the holy people, but by the political people. This propaganda led to the terrible Persecutions in Europe, the so-called Burning Time. Nine million people were killed, possibly more, over a period of three hundred years. That's where the term "Witch hunt" comes from. And on a small scale, it happened again in this country, in Salem. And all that stuff about Witches and devils and negative magic (what they called "Black Magic") — that is not true, that was all invented. It has nothing to do with us, and it's very important that we keep emphasizing that. I also think we should work to make sure that there's no danger.

Q: Can you comment on the belief that's very prevalent today about creating your own reality, extending to choosing your own parents or choosing an illness?

A: That can get very, very fishy. OK. That has been so misinterpreted, and in a way that is so cruel. The concept of choosing your own reality, especially in terms of illness, has been misunderstood. Well, first of all, choosing your own reality is very helpful in daily life, because we know that we're in our own reality now, we know what we are involved with now, and the next step is knowing that since we chose it, we can change it. It's very good for times when a person is trying to heal himself or herself, because it gives you the strength to know, "I can choose to draw and manifest everything I need to myself, to help myself get well." But there can't be any *blame*, you see? What has been very cruel, has been a misunderstanding of the concept of karma, using blame.

When I used to do my radio show, during Vietnam and just after it — when I would start talking about choosing your own reality, people would call me up and say, "You mean those people chose to be bombed and hurt or killed?" Well no, I don't mean that at all. I know it's been very misunderstood, but here's what I mean: We can't prove what happened in other lifetimes. We don't even know for sure that there *were* other lifetimes. How are you going to prove it? People are feeling guilty because they were told they were terrible people in other lives; that is such a waste of guilt! It's possible, but this stuff really can't be proved. The so-called information about past lives can only guide us. But — when we believe that we did choose our own parents and basic life circumstances when we were in the Invisible World, if we use that as a *metaphor* — it's very helpful. It takes a lot of the edge off any early negative experience. If you stop and think about it: "Well, if I chose this, I must have done this for a reason. Now, let me work it through. Let me deal with this."

We say today — those of us who are Witches — we chose to be born into this time because this is a changing time, and we can share our information with the world that seems to need it, especially in terms of the environment and with women's rights. So when we can say that we chose to born in this time — that can be meaningful and helpful. What's bad is when blame comes in. What those who talk about karma and reincarnation in a blameworthy way don't know, is that in this form of Witchcraft and occult studies — there is no blame and there is no guilt! That is out! *There is personal responsibility only.* I do believe that there are people who were born into — let's not say "born into," let's say *went into* — dangerous or harmful circumstances, because they felt vulnerable. Not because they were bad, not because they were stupid, but because they felt vulnerable. And a lot of the information that's coming out today about co-dependency supports this. Often people will constantly re-create abusive situations in their lives. Not because they're stupid, not because they're bad, but because they feel vulnerable to those situations, and they have no other models. I believe this could hold true for lifetime-to-lifetime circumstances as well.

Karma is a very complicated subject, and I go into it in a long chapter in POSITIVE MAGIC.[4] Also, what we say is: once you become aware of personal responsibility and getting rid of blame and guilt, then it is your responsibility to help others. Because you have that awareness, it's your job to help others. And none of that stuff about "It's their karma, leave them to suffer," which is... here I'm saying "no blame and no guilt," but it makes me so angry when I hear that. Especially in the New Age community; if some people have studied for maybe five minutes, then they think they understand something.

Q: When you were just talking about not putting the blame on other people...

A: Or on yourself.

Q: And you have to take responsibility — since you are a Witch, do you have to take the responsibility to pass it on?

---

4 See "Karma and Reincarnation" in POSITIVE MAGIC, Chapter Five.

A: Well, there are a million little ways you can help people other than to "hit them over the head" with Witchcraft. I don't go around telling people I'm a Witch unless it's appropriate. But I try to help people. And I think we all do — in our own way. And one thing we do is this thing we call "witnessing." Now, of course, there's *free will* and *for the good of all,* and you can witness a person suffering and not know whether you should do magic to help them...but what I always do is, I do magic for them. But I always say, "according to free will and for the good of all." So there are a lot of ways to help people other than to tell them you're a Witch and here's the truth. Because everybody thinks their religion is the best, and it's always possible that we're wrong. They could come down in a UFO with the Religion of Zog, and *that* could turn out to be the best religion in the universe! Then we'll all look like jerks.

Q: Marion, I'm not very clear on the concept of All Time, past, present, and future being "Now." Can you elaborate on this a little bit?

A: OK. First of all, this is an idea which abounds in the New Physics. Now, it's an old occult concept also, that "All Time is *Now.*" It's very hard to explain, but it comes to you. Really — it'll hit you as I keep talking. Now: Past has already happened. It only exists in your mind, right? In your perception. Future hasn't happened yet. But both of them are here, because your mind is here.

50

That's it, right? You got it! OK. I don't get any credit for your getting that. You get all the credit!

The Holidays

A wonderful source of power and magic for anyone to enjoy today is the celebration of the Witchcraft holidays. In modern times, we call them the Witchcraft, Pagan or occult holidays, because they are traditionally associated with magic. But in ancient times, they were simply the *holy days* or *Sabbats.* In pre Judeo-Christian Europe, everyone celebrated these days. They were a critically important part of daily life.

The Words *Magic* and *Pagan*

The holidays remain from a time when magic wasn't considered anything extraordinary, but was as common as prayer is today. I define magic as *transformation —* change — created on purpose, by personal skill. The practice of magic is *ritual and celebration with intention to create change.* Everyone practiced magic in early Europe — for reasons that were not only spiritual, but practical.

In the Neo-Pagan movement, we have reclaimed the word Pagan as something to be proud of, but the original meaning of the word had no perjorative overtones at all. That came much later. The word "Pagan" simply means "of the country." This refers to the fact that the people in

European cities and towns embraced the "modern" religion of Christianity much earlier than did their country cousins. By the Fourteenth Century, powerful rulers had forced Europe to become officially Christian, and any practice of the old ways was forbidden. Since the celebration of these holidays persisted for the longest time in country areas of every part of Europe, the holidays became known as Pagan. Anyone and anything Pagan was considered socially and politically unacceptable. The same negative connotation applied to the word "heathen," which literally means "people who live in the heath" (English country areas). In fact, these holidays are *still* celebrated in all Western countries today — always in rural regions, where people's lives are more directly influenced by nature. These are basically nature holidays, having to do with the powerful effects of the seasons on agriculture.

The Wheel

The calendar we use today is called the Gregorian Calendar; first introduced in 1582 C.E. It is *solar* — based on the movements of the sun. Using this calendar, today we visualize each year as a flat rectangle, as you can see when you look at your own calendar on your desk or wall. But for countless ages before this one, the calendar was *lunar*, based on the moon — and based on the image of the year as a giant wheel. Each year was visualized as a circle which spun slowly clockwise, like the sun. The holidays were seen as eight spokes on the Wheel Of The Year. Each spoke represented a turning point from one season into another. And, as mentioned earlier, the name for the Wheel of the Year was the *Yule*.

If you stop and think about it, the shape in which you visualize your year determines how you relate to the concept of time, and consequently how time affects your entire life. The modern year is seen as rectangular and static, and we see ourselves as somewhat detached from it. So time can seem to be a force existing somehow outside of ourselves, exerting its mysterious power over us. However, the ancient Pagan year is seen as a constantly turning circle. It is, in fact, a portrait of our planet Earth — *with us on it*. The turning motion of the year is *part* of its identity, not separate from it. The cyclical, circular motion of time is *part of our identity* , too — because we live on the Wheel, we stand in the circle. This is one important reason why most Witchcraft magic — in fact most magic of any kind — is accomplished within a circle. The circle reflects the ancient view of self in relation to the world, a concept which is a source of tremendous power.

Today, many people are afraid of time, and much of our culture is based on denying its passage. But in ancient times, people saw themselves as integrally connected to the passing of time, and this connection was a comforting fact of the human condition. The passing of time was seen as eternal: Every ending led to a new beginning, and even death was seen as part of an endless, totally connected cycle.

Nothing could be more important to an ancient Pagan than the changing of the seasons — which determined when to plant, when to sow, when to harvest, and when to make preparations to move indoors for the long, cold winter. Everyone's lives depended directly on agriculture, and the holidays told everyone each phase of their crops' progress. Even illiterate people could count days and nights. The sequence of the holidays was absolutely dependable. If, for example, the entire village had just celebrated Halloween, which is the final harvest, everyone knew that exactly six weeks later would come the Midwinter Solstice, which meant — among other things — the total dead of winter. Food and kindling wood would have to be stocked in adequate supply, along with candles, warm clothing, blankets, and whatever else was needed in order to move indoors for several months. Life depended on the holidays, and the holidays represented life.

Just like other ancient mysteries, such as Stonehenge and the Giant Pyramids — the holidays were planned in a surprisingly sophisticated and learned way, indicating high intelligence and scholarship among people who were supposedly primitive (by today's standards). The holidays were determined astronomically. Of course in those days, astronomy included astrology, but both are based on the accurate movement of the planets, which actually seems to have been known when the holidays were first celebrated — over twelve thousand years ago!

The Spokes of the Wheel

On the Wheel of The year, four spokes are the two Equinoxes and the two Solstices:

- The Vernal or Spring Equinox, which always occurs March 20-23
- The Autumnal or Fall Equinox, always Sept. 20-23
- The Midsummer Solstice, always June 20-23
- The Midwinter Solstice, always Dec. 20-23.

The Equinoxes and Solstices occur on any one of the four days indicated; the exact date (and time) varies each year. This is because the holidays have been translated from the earlier lunar calendar to our modern solar one. On the ancient lunar calendar, they would of course have been consistent.

Today, the Equinoxes and Solstices are often recognized as "weather holidays." Watching the news on television, the weatherperson is the one who reminds us, "Today is officially the first day of Fall," or whichever time has arrived. Our lives may no longer directly depend on this information, but it still is a meaningful announcement for our psyches.

The remaining four spokes on the Wheel are the Cross-Quarter days, the days which fall exactly (on our modern calendar, almost exactly) in between the Equinoxes and Solstices.

The Cross-Quarter days are:

- Halloween, Oct. 31
- Candlemas, Feb. 2
- Beltane, May 1
- Lammas, Aug. 2.

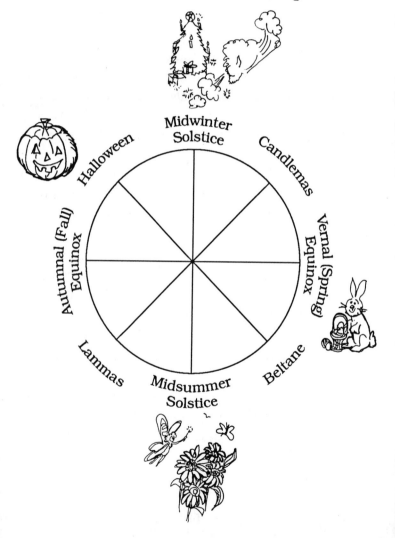

Looking at the dates of these holidays, you will notice that major Jewish and Christian holidays fall close to these times, sometimes right on the same day. The Jewish calendar is still lunar, which partially explains this. Another explanation is that all of our holidays — Jewish and Christian as well as Pagan — have common roots: *the seasons.*

Equally important: The meaning and symbolism of each Jewish and Christian holiday are very similar to that of the neighboring Pagan holiday. This symbolism is so deeply imbedded in the human psyche that no laws, either political or religious, could stop people from celebrating the original holidays. The names of the holidays were changed, the dates were moved — slightly — and the Judeo-Christian meanings were woven into the Pagan meanings which would not die.

The Celebrations

In ancient times, every family celebrated each holiday with its region, or village. Witches celebrated in covens (small groups), and often the covens joined the larger village celebrations. Sometimes the Witches led the celebrations, sometimes village elders did, sometimes the Druids, and quite possibly also sometimes other magicians and magical folk, whose names have been lost in the centuries since the Medieval Persecutions.

Today, when I hold group rituals, I say they are "non-sectarian," but they are actually "*pre*-sectarian." They come from a time when all religion was related to one spiritual theme — nature — and this theme was considered at once Divine and practical. The groups which celebrated this theme all celebrated in similar ways, based on shared core beliefs. The groups were not seen as different from one another, but rather closely related. These were Pagan times.

My emphasis today is on *retranslation* of the holidays and of the beliefs which they represent — because I believe that the meanings of these times (at once Divine and practical) still hold limitless riches for our lives. In fact, the meanings of these times may even hold the keys for survival of our planet. After all, the holidays are based on the turning of the Earth, and on reverence for all of nature. Isn't reverence for nature (as an actual, deeply held belief, not as a superficial, politically correct stance) desperately needed today? Many so-called "primitive" native people still base their spiritual life on this reverence for nature, and celebrate similar holidays — which they never lost. I feel it is time that we in the so-called modern West rediscover the power and beauty of our own all-but-lost holidays.

Celebrating Today

In more ancient times, when everyone's lives depended on agriculture, the ways in which the holidays coincided with phases of the crops was so obvious that the celebration of each of these times was automatically laden with specific meaning, which was obvious to everyone. Now, when the holidays come around, we might have to remind ourselves of their significance. Actually, in a more urban society, I think we need the magic of the holidays more than ever, to help us reconnect to our roots in the Earth.

Whether we are Witches, Pagans or members of any religion or even no religion at all, we can still celebrate by simply stopping our activities for a time, lighting a candle, looking out a window, and meditating on the changing season and its importance in our lives. Even this is a significant way to partake of the magic of a holiday — to pause and simply acknowledge its presence. We could go further and meet in small family and communal groups, as in ancient times. However, now we also realize we are a global village, so we may include this understanding in our celebrations. If you can't put aside the time to mark the holiday — especially in a group of people — exactly on the holiday itself, you might prefer to work on the weekend closest to that time. Many groups do this, feeling it's more important to get together and share the occasion rather than be rigid about working magic at any specific moment. This is helpful to remember for the Equinoxes and the Solstices, which are astronomical events that actually occur at specific moments. Often we are asleep at those times, or otherwise engaged, so we may simply wait until we are free either to meet with others, or really have the time to work magic, meditate — or even pray — alone. Sometimes it's easier to do this work just *before* the holiday. None of this really matters; as long as we really do acknowledge the holiday in some fashion, we will be enriched by it. Precise times of each holiday up until the year 2000 are given at the end of this chapter.

On radio, I used to say, when you celebrate a holiday, simply use the *imagery of crops* in your daily lives. We all have crops: family, projects, work, art, relationships, etc. Use the seasonal rhythms to relate to these crops just as the ancient Pagans did — such as which times to plant, to nurture, to harvest, and to plan. This imagery still applies, as we will see as we go through the Wheel of The Year, and note the meaning of each holiday.

For those of us who are Witches and Pagans, the holidays are not only times to celebrate and draw upon with the imagery of crops; they are also traditional times to work magic. Even for those who work magic in a solitary way, remember you are not really alone, because you are joining with many other Witches, Pagans and positive magicians who also work at these times.

The ways in which you choose to work magic are of course, up to you; I include numerous suggestions in my other books, always emphasizing the importance of keeping your work non-manipulative — *for the good of all and according to free will.* These principles are necessary not only in the content of your work, but in the *style* of your work as well. For example, never insist that a member of your group work any magic, or even say any words, that he or she feels uncomfortable about. The secret of a successful coven is that there is always room for everyone to follow his or her heart honestly. As magical religions gain more and more popularity, there may be a tendency for ego trips or power plays to distort the work; in other words, Witches and

64

Pagans could fall prey to the very same pitfalls that have distorted some areas of the more traditional religions.

It is important to remember that in Witchcraft, Paganism and Goddess Religion, the connection to Deity comes from within. No one can tell you how to worship, how to celebrate, how to work magic, or how to create a ritual. You can share the process of discovery with others, and you can choose to take suggestions and guidelines from many sources (including my work), but the bottom line is that all of us must ultimately discover and create our own theology. This is a joyous, empowering process which has been denied most of humankind for thousands of years. I feel very strongly about this, so I am purposely not providing any specific instructions here for celebrating the holidays, but only providing the broadest guidelines. Discover, invent and synthesize for yourself!

And if you wish to remain within a more traditional Judeo-Christian mode and still want to enjoy the holidays, please do so. Find a way which is personally meaningful to you, to incorporate the rich poetry of the seasons with your own Deity and your own prayers and practices. The holidays can be truly non-sectarian.

The Holidays

The Eight Great Holidays are always six weeks apart.

Halloween — October 31st

Halloween is the most famous Pagan holiday known to the "outside" world. In fact, many people think it is the only one (not realizing it is one of eight)! Halloween is a Cross-Quarter Day; it is the third and final harvest of the year, after which the fields were prepared for a winter's rest. The last of the year's crops were gathered, with thanksgiving for the harvest. This occurs in the sign of Scorpio, which rules death and rebirth. Halloween is believed to be ruled by The Male God in His underworld aspect, and also by the Crone aspect of The Goddess.

As discussed earlier, the ancient Celtic name for Halloween is *Samhain* (thought by some to be pronounced "Sow-winn"). The word Halloween literally means "Holy Evening."

Halloween has another deep meaning in the magical traditions. It heralds the coming of Winter as a time when the sun retreats, and darkness approaches in the form of longer nights and colder days. In nature, this is also a time of death; leaves, plants and insects die and disappear into the ground. So Halloween focuses on death, but it does so by celebrating the eternity of life in general, and reincarnation in particular. Perhaps no holiday so clearly illustrates the Pagan belief that death and rebirth are intertwined. On this night, the "veil between the worlds" is said to be thin, and we can communicate most easily with our loved ones who have moved on to the other side. Non-Pagans and non-Witches may find this a frightening concept, when actually it is meant to be comforting for all concerned. Halloween is also the New Year for many Witches.

In the Catholic religion, November 1, the day after Halloween, is called *All Souls' Day* or *All Saints' Day,* dedicated to the holy spirits of the departed. In South America, this is the *Day of The Dead,* when people commune with the spirits of their ancestors with such customs as picnicking at cemeteries, and dancing in the streets dressed as skeletons and ghosts. On a more sombre note, the Jewish Yom Kippur, which occurs several weeks earlier, includes a New Year celebration when the dead are honored — with an emphasis on ancestors and family loved ones — and the principle of eternal life is acknowledged. Cemeteries are visited, prayers are offered in the temple, and memorial candles are lit at home. In North America, the final harvest is celebrated as Thanksgiving, a time of feasting and brotherhood, with tradition linking Christian Pilgrims to Native Americans.

To a Witch, none of this seems very different from our own Halloween.

Some Other Halloween Customs

In pre-Christian Europe, Halloween was celebrated with bonfires and games of divination. Witches traveled to their meetings on foot, carrying candles to light the way; and to protect the flame from the wind, the candles were placed in hallowed-out gourds. Gourds, like pumpkins, are a seasonal crop in the squash family. Eventually, faces were carved in the gourds, which evolved into our familiar jack o' lanterns.

For your modern Halloween — this is a wonderful time to give thanks for the harvest of your own "crops" in your life. This is a good time to remember loved ones on the other side, and even be open to messages — if this is your belief — or simply happy memories, if you are less literal. This is a time to prepare for Winter. We may not have to stock up on candles, warm clothing and food any longer, but we can prepare ourselves psychologically. This is a time to look within one's self, for that deep connection with our Deities which provides a light to sustain us through the darkness of the coming winter months. It is a time of turning inward, a period of planning and reassessment.

In a lighter vein, light a candle in a jolly pumpkin or gourd, and make a wish (non-manipulative, of course) for the Winter months ahead. Since this is traditionally the evening to use divination (looking into the future and into other realms), it is an excellent occasion to use tarot cards, the I Ching or your pendulum or crystal ball.[1]

On radio, I always held a giant "Genuine Ancient/ Modern Non-Sectarian" Halloween ritual at midnight, in which all the listeners could join. As long as I can remember, Halloween has always been my favorite holiday.

---

[1] For instructions on divination, specifically tarot cards and the I Ching, see Chapter Seven in POSITIVE MAGIC. For instructions for using the pendulum, see page 16 in EARTH MAGIC).

The Midwinter Solstice — December 20th-23rd

This holiday is the shortest day and the longest night of the year, and marks the passage of the Sun from Sagittarius into Capricorn. On the Wheel of The Year, the Midwinter Solstice stands exactly opposite the Midsummer Solstice. Interestingly enough, this holiday is named for the Wheel itself; Yule is the ancient name for this day, and "Yuletide" means "Yule time," or the *Time of the Wheel.*

In early Europe, this holiday signified the rebirth of the sun in the sky. Bleak and dreary winter days grow shorter and shorter; and in an earlier time without electric lights, it seemed as if the sun were actually going to eventually disappear. So on the day when the sun began to grow brighter — and the days longer — there was much cause for celebration and renewed optimism. Many of the ageless Yuletide images and customs have to do with rebirth and cheer, using Pagan symbolism. This is the time of the Birth of the Sun (Son).

Trees were sacred to many Pagan sects, including Druids, so the Yule log was burned in every hearth, and a segment of it was kept burning to bring good fortune all through the ensuing year. Red candles represented the sun in the sky. Holly branches and mistletoe were (and still are) sacred to The Goddess. A tree representing The Tree of Life was brought indoors, and decked with round discs and candles (the sun again), as well as sweets to ensure a sweet year. Gifts were exchanged, and ceremonial cakes and ale added to the feast of celebration.

69

Incidentally, the giant monument of Stonehenge was built for the Solstice; the Sun casts the shadow of the outer stone on the center altar stone at the exact moment of Midwinter. Some experts believe this is the primary purpose of this giant monument.

Obviously, many popular Yuletide customs remained into Christian times, and were added to the religious celebrations of Christmas. I suspect this is true for the holiday of Hannukah also. The Tree of Life can be found in the study of Jewish mysticism, *The Kaballah*. Hannukah always occurs very close to the Solstice, and candles and gifts (specifically for children) are an important part of this celebration, which is also called *The Festival of Lights.*

On radio, I always used to remind people that the so-called "Holiday Depression" which so many seem to suffer from at this season is not new. Perhaps an element of it is new — a dissatisfaction with the hollowness and crass commercialism of a religious time — but the sense of darkness and accompanying vague despair is as old as our Pagan forbears in nearly forgotten winters long ago. What cheered them was the return of the sun, and their celebration of this. So I have always recommended to everyone: celebrate the Midwinter Solstice! Acknowledge that at this magical and sacred moment, the sun is returning and Spring is on its way; and plug into the good magic of all the Witches, Pagans and Druids who are working at this time. This is a time-honored and effective way to beat the holiday blues, and I always felt it should be public knowledge.

For your modern Yule celebration, draw upon as much of the ancient imagery as you wish. This is a time of rest and turning inward, a time to reassess your crops from the last Harvest, and to plan your crops for the year ahead.

In my coven, we share a holiday meal and exchange gifts. Goddess knows that seasonal Yuletide decorations — pinecones, evergreen foliage and trees — are not hard to find in modern times, even in the heart of the city! We decorate "Solstice trees" (which actually look a lot like Christmas trees) and prefer living trees to cut ones, given the state of the modern environment. Small evergreen trees may be purchased in pots, and if you use one, it's important to select an appropriate place to plant your tree outdoors in the months to come.

The important thing to remember on this holiday, is that the sun will come back, that Spring and Summer will really follow again. This is not only a fact of nature, but also a powerful metaphor for our lives. This celebration cheered people up, back when cheer was hard to come by — and it can cheer people up now as well. Even if you also celebrate Christmas or Hannukah, I recommend that you take time to mark the Midwinter Solstice, as close to the exact moment of its occurrence as you can. Light a red candle, look up at the sky and welcome the sun's return — a truly non-sectarian thought.

Candlemas — February 2nd

Candlemas is a Cross-Quarter Day, and occurs in the sign of Aquarius. This is the earliest beginning of Spring

— under the ground. In Jungian psychology, a wonderful word is used to refer to these first stirrings of life, which take place underground, almost hidden, in darkness; the word is *cthonic.* This is the time when the first seeds of the season begin to grow — imperceptibly — deep within the Earth. In Ireland, this holiday is known as St. Bridget's (or Brigid's) Day; Bridget was a Catholic saint, and also is an ancient name for the Goddess. In most of the West, Candlemas has survived as Ground Hog Day. Old names for this day are *Imbolc,* and *The Feast of the Waxing Light.*

Candlemas is celebrated by those who know nothing of Witchcraft tradition, as "Groundhog Day." This is the day when a little creature stirs beneath the earth and comes up to tell us about Spring. The belief is that if the groundhog sees its shadow, a warm spring will be early. If it returns to its burrow, Spring will be cold and late. This is an uninformed remnant of the awareness of seeds stirring underground.

The seeds stirring underground are metaphors for the stirrings of our own crops being born again in our lives. Candlemas is traditionally a time to banish the darkness and cold of Winter, by lighting candles and planning exactly how, when and what to plant. Use Candlemas to banish the darkness of Winter in your own lives; light candles to herald The Goddess's rule of Spring, and plan your crops carefully. Nurture those that have already begun to stir.

The Vernal, or Spring Equinox — March 20th-23rd

The Spring Equinox marks the exact moment of equal day and equal night on this planet. Equinox means "equal night," and Vernal means "Spring." The Vernal Equinox stands opposite the Autumnal Equinox on the Wheel calendar. It is the astrological turning point from Pisces to Aries. At an Equinox, everything stands in total balance: equal day and equal night, equal light and equal darkness, equal male and female forces in nature, equal Goddess and God, equal sun and moon influences as well. This is the First Planting, of what modern gardeners call "cold weather crops;" the hardiest crops of the year have always been planted at this time.

The Spring Equinox also celebrates the fertility of animals. The first baby rabbits are born at this time, as are the first lambs, and the first eggs are laid by domestic and wild birds. The Christian holiday of Easter occurs on the first Sunday after the first Full Moon after the Vernal Equinox of every year.[2] Popular imagery of Easter includes: the Easter Bunny, Easter eggs, Easter baskets and even the Easter Lamb (as dinner). All of this comes from ancient celebrations of the Spring Equinox. In Judaism, the Equinox influences two holidays which occur around this time: Passover and Purim. Passover has a traditional lamb dinner (the so-called "Paschal Lamb"), and uses a boiled egg as part of the dinner ritual.

---

[2]For an excellent discussion of the Pagan origins of Easter customs, see Pauline Campanelli's *The Wheel of The Year*, Llewellyn Publications, St. Paul, 1989, p.67.

Purim celebrates a Biblical heroine named Esther — a name which sounds a lot like Easter. Both probably grew out of the ancient name for The Goddess of Spring — *Eshtar*, recently discovered by archaeologists in Syria (other pronunciations include *Ostara* and *Ishtar*).[3]

For your modern Vernal Equinox celebration — this is the First Planting: the time to plant your earliest and hardiest crops. Many self-help experts suggest that the easiest tasks of a project be accomplished first, working up to the more difficult ones with time. This is one possible metaphor for the "hardiest" crops. The first crops could also be whatever you consider to be the first phase of any endeavor. In the garden, the traditional crop to plant at this time is peas. Other seeds, flower and vegetable, can be sprouted indoors for the Second Planting outdoors later on. As an animal lover, I care for animals all year round; but Spring Equinox is a special time to show our love for animals, specifically baby animals — not by eating them! — but by helping them, perhaps with a donation to an animal charity. Seasonal decorations of flowers, specifically the kind we can grow indoors, help bring the spirit of The Goddess of Spring into our homes.

Beltane — May 1st

This holiday celebrates the ascendancy of the female principle in nature — The Goddess — and takes place in the astrological sign of Taurus. It is the Second Planting,

---

[3] Merlin Stone

a time of sowing and planting seeds and seedlings, as well as a celebration of the flowering of earlier crops. A major fertility holiday, Beltane is considered an excellent time for human conception. In fact, the idea of people conceiving children at the same time that crops are planted, is a time-honored connection. Each activity was believed to aid the other, and to be reflected by nature's bounty, healthy livestock and healthy babies.

In pre-Christian Europe, sexual activity was considered sacred, and Beltane was literally a night of love. Women and men met in the dark, and paired off under sacred groves of trees, or lay on the newly-sown fields. This was believed to create healthy babies, and simultaneously provide a blessing for the crops. Any child conceived on Beltane Eve was considered a child of The Goddess and The God. All such children were given the last name "Robinson," which means *child of The God,* and considered special. The names Robin and Marian were folk names for The God and The Goddess. Many villages chose a King and Queen of the May, which were actually honorary Priest and Priestess positions for the holiday.

Beltane was also celebrated with Maypole dances by day and bonfires by night. The Maypole, a tall pole festooned with long ribbons, is both a phallic fertility symbol and a Springtime representation of the Tree of Life. Oatmeal cakes are traditional Beltane food. In Germany, the holiday is called Walpurgis Night, and even in Russia it is still celebrated — as Mayday.

One ancient Beltane ritual involved "riding" a broom,

and leaping over the freshly-sown fields as a fertility blessing. In modern covens, we take turns riding a broom and leaping over a houseplant. This is still a blessed time to conceive a child.

Suggested ways to celebrate Beltane today: use the imagery of planting and sowing seeds for your own crops: relationships, projects, work and family. Since this is the Second Planting, you might be able to follow up with the next phases of projects begun at the Spring Equinox. — but of course, any planting (beginning) is appropriate now. If you have a garden, plant your warm weather crops (hot weather crops must come a few weeks later in the Northern hemisphere). This is a propitious time to focus on love relationships and children. If you have a Beltane celebration, decorate with seasonal flowers — and don't forget the oatmeal cookies!

The Midsummer Solstice — June 20th-23rd

This is the longest day and the shortest night of the year, and stands exactly opposite the Midwinter Solstice on the Wheel. It marks the turning point from the astrological sign of Gemini into Cancer. It is a celebration of the male principle in nature, The God — so in folkloric texts we see a lot of sun imagery such as flaming wooden discs, wheels of fire, and flaming hoops being rolled downhill into lakes and streams. People danced around bonfires, and the fires themselves were considered lucky this night, so bits of flaming wood embers were brought home to the family hearth. The heat and full flowering of summer is at its peak. This holiday marks the Third Planting.

The Midsummer Solstice was honored by Shakespeare in A MIDSUMMER NIGHT'S DREAM— and more recently by Woody Allen in his A MIDSUMMER NIGHT'S SEX COMEDY. Both scenarios involve the themes of sexual liaisons, identity switches, magic and fairies — all traditional for this time. The "little folk" are believed to be out dancing on this short night.

Suggested ways to celebrate the Midsummer Solstice today: This is a time to nurture our personal crops of all kinds — already sown but not yet harvested, as well as a time to plant new ones. It is a time to make changes, to reassess, make adjustments and appreciate our accomplishments. In modern gardens, this is still the Third Planting, so it's a good time to plant Fall vegetables. In your celebrations, use seasonal flowers and grasses, and candles — carefully, of course.

Lammas — August 2nd

Lammas is a Cross-Quarter Day, and the First Harvest of year; it occurs in the sign of Leo. Even though Lammas seems to take place at the very peak of Summer, to the ancient Pagan it meant the beginning of Fall. Many crops were gathered at Lammas, but the one crop which this holiday celebrates most is the harvest of the grain. This meant, in various places, corn, wheat, millet, rye and barley. The aspects of The Goddess most popularly associated with the grain harvest are Ceres and Demeter.

An ancient custom to celebrate Lammas was not only the harvesting of the grain, but the grinding of it and the baking of the bread. Loaves of bread baked at this time were considered sacred.

We always celebrate a harvest by giving thanks to The Goddess and The God for our crops — including thoughts, relationships, ideas, projects and families. This does not mean that we have to stop planting (initiating things), nor does it mean we have to consider our crops completed; as always, we work with the seasonal metaphors as best we can. The metaphor for Lammas is literally counting our blessings. As we take the time to appreciate our harvest and its Divine source, we provide the foundation for future harvests. In our own celebrations, freshly baked bread, preferably whole grain, is a delicious way to acknowledge the power of Lammas. Seasonal fruits, vegetables and herbs are also in order, and late Summer flowers can brighten our homes.

The Autumnal, or Fall Equinox-September 20th-23rd

The Fall Equinox is the Second Harvest of the year, and literally means "equal night." It marks the transition from Virgo to Libra. As stated earlier, an Equinox is a time of balance and harmony in all things. This is the time when everything stands in perfect balance just before Winter — equal day and equal night, equal dark and equal light, equal sun and equal moon, equal male and equal female influences in nature. This holiday stands exactly opposite the Vernal, or Spring Equinox on the Wheel of The Year.

The Jewish holiday of Succoth falls either exactly on the Autumnal Equinox or close to it. Succoth is also a harvest holiday of thanksgiving for crops. In modern Western lore the "Harvest Moon" is the Full Moon closest to this Equinox.

Suggested ways to celebrate the Autumnal Equinox today: In Pagan and Witchcraft belief, on every harvest holiday, it is traditional to *give thanks* for all crops, all abundance which we have achieved up until this point. Think about your crops, which may be projects, family, loved ones, friends, and accomplishments of various kinds. Also, focus on the principles of balance, harmony and equality. It is an excellent time to work magic for social justice and fairness, racial and sexual equality — anything having to do with these principles. Celebrate with seasonal vegetables, herbs and fruits as well as flowers. In the garden, this is a true harvest and a time to can, preserve, or freeze some of the bounty — and share it with others.

Conclusion

As we tune into the traditional times of the holidays, we are joining with all of the thousands of Witches and positive magicians who work and have worked magic at these times. At the very least, our lives are enriched, and we feel connected to the Earth and the turning of the seasons in a profound and meaningful way — even in the heart of a big city. But if we take these occasions even more seriously, and choose our magic (or prayers) carefully, we are helped by the powerful seasonal energy shifts on our planet; we can make huge and positive changes in our own lives as well as helping others. And remember — on all the holidays it is important to send blessings to the larger community: our world.

Epilogue

This is how we ended the evening: We held an Ancient/Modern Halloween Ritual. I had planned ahead of time that this ritual would not be taped, assuming that in the audience — which had now become the magic circle — there would be people who wanted to celebrate this religious event in privacy. If there was even one person who felt this way, I wanted to honor that. However, I can share the ritual now with everyone who reads this book. Perhaps it will serve as a helpful guide for your own Halloween rituals.

The ritual we celebrated that night was an outgrowth — another version and an interpretation — of the Halloween ritual I always led on radio. My radio ritual was, in fact, the source of the term "Ancient/Modern," because over the years I would always strive to connect that which was most ancient — public, communal ritual — with that which was so modern: FM radio. I would promo the event as *The Ancient/Modern Non-Sectarian Genuine Halloween Ritual.* And so it was at Speak Easy.

On radio, we always began the ritual at midnight, the so-called "Witching Hour." I have never quite understood the significance of using the word Witch as a verb, but I have always acknowledged the mystical meaning of midnight. It comes from the Kabbalah, and signifies the one moment that stands suspended between the forces of justice and mercy. It is traditionally an effective time to work magic.

However, at Speak Easy, we began the ritual at a little after 10 pm, immediately following the lecture. This was for the convenience of all present, since it was a week night. This was not a problem, since on Halloween, the entire evening has magical power.

I am always aware that no matter where this ritual is performed, no matter what the circumstances — the most important, vital thing to remember is the heart of the meaning of Halloween.

Halloween, or Samhain, means:
• Literally, "Holy Evening"
• The Witches' New Year, so a time of new beginnings
• The Third and Final Harvest of the Year
• A time that the Veil (Between the Worlds) is thin, and loved ones from the other side can join in
• A time when death and rebirth are celebrated as a continuum
• A time to deal with reincarnation
• And mainly, a time to work magic.

In our Halloween magic we include:
• the work of Wish Fulfillment — for each individual
• and, of course, that mainstay of ancient communal

ritual — Blessing the Community.   Today this
means the global community, as well as the imme-
diate one (in our case, New York City).

We had supplied the following ritual objects for each
person:
- a donut, to represent Earth
- apple cider, to represent Water
- incense, to represent Air
- a candle, to represent Fire.

Actually, there wasn't a separate amount of incense
for everyone, so we shared mine. The four ritual objects
could have been any cookie or cake, any drink, any
fragrance (even perfume or talcum powder — *if* you like
the smell!), and any candle that has either not been
used at all, or has only been used for positive purposes.
If any or even all of the objects is missing, I always say you
can instead *visualize* the object, and use it from the
Invisible Realm.

Since we didn't tape the ritual, I will reconstruct it
here. That evening, I led the work, by making most of the
spoken statements.   In one's own coven, either a leader
can be chosen or several can take turns.

And oh, yes — since it's non-sectarian, you really
don't actually have to be a Witch to celebrate either this
ritual or a variation on it!

Everyone was seated at their tables as we began,

simply because of considerations of space. We had thought the space was a large one, but we had at least 150 people present, and that felt a bit crowded.

I remained on stage, lit my candle, raised my Athamé, and spoke the following — or at least something close to it. I am a big advocate of improvised ritual for most occasions. Certain principles must be included,[1] but the rest is up to you...

---

[1] As outlined in Chapter Eight, "Words of Power" in POSITIVE MAGIC, and page 15 in MAGIC FOR PEACE.

The Ancient/Modern Halloween Ritual

I hereby consecrate this work
To The Goddess and The God, and the work of Positive Magic only.
We call upon The Goddess and The God
And the One Power working for and through us all
To bless us on this night of Power, on this Samhain, this Halloween.
This work is for the good of all only;
This work is according to free will only.
We stand Between The Worlds —
The World of Form
And The Invisible Realm
We call upon The Goddess and The God to work for and through us all,
to guide our work and make it manifest.
We invite our loved ones in the Invisible Realm
to join with us in joyous celebration.

All: *Welcome, welcome, Blessed Be!*

We are all divinely protected and perfectly safe.
On this Third and Final Harvest of the year,
We think of all our blessings,
And give thanks —
and on this thanks our future harvests will be built.
The Elements support us in our work.

We light the incense

All: *Air!*

We light the candle

All: *Fire!*

We eat the cake

All: *Earth!*

We drink the drink

All: *Water!*

(A brief pause for chewing, swallowing, drinking)

And now the wish:
In silence we each form our wish.
Each wish supports every other wish.
We each manifest our own wish,
And also know that every other one comes true

All: *Comes true!*

(Silence as the wishes are thought)

The Goddess and The God work for and through us all

to make each wish come true.
And now we bless our community, New York City
(here, fill in your own),
And all who live in it,
For safety, protection, abundance, health and peace.
Turning now, to our village,
our Global Village, Earth —
We bless this planet, our home,
and every being on it
for fairness and karmic justice
peace and protection
an end to hunger, war and danger
and replace this with peace and safety, plenty,
healing, love and protection for all
for every being, every life form —
and even though this may seem impossible,
the problems are all solved
In all time and all space.
This is a doorway for The Goddess and The God to
come through.

And so mote it be.

All: *And so mote it be!*

(Blow out candles)

Everybody dance! Clockwise of course!

The magic circle dance is a very important part of this ritual, since it both raises and then releases the energies. Everybody got up from their tables with much scraping of chairs, and, holding hands, formed a circle — which was almost impossible in that darkened, crowded space. But we did it. On the sound system we played our tape of "Halloween City,"[2] and everybody at first sort of shuffled and then actually danced clockwise. I was holding hands in the circle too, with people I'd never met before, although I saw plenty of familiar faces here and there. For the first time, then, I saw the costumes — many were medieval.

At the finish of the song, there was much hugging and many wishes of Happy New Year. I cannot possibly tell you how inspiring, connecting, rewarding and comforting this ritual is. If you do it, you will feel this for yourself, in your own way and on your own terms.

When we left Speak Easy later that night, the Village Parade had ended, although many costumed people still strolled the streets. Did they know why they were in costume, why they still wanted to share the night? Did they feel the power of those mythic truths, the true meaning of Halloween, which hundreds of years of patriarchal monotheism could not eradicate nor put to rest? In any case, they had celebrated something — communally — and that is at least half of the ancient part of Halloween.

---

[2] The song, "Halloween City" is available on audio tape from Earth Magic Productions, on a 2-song cassingle POSITIVE MAGIC: THE MUSIC.

We took the leftover apples, donuts and cider, with napkins and cups, and left it all for the homeless people living in the Port Authority Bus Terminal. We put an invisible blessing on this Harvest, and returned to our own homes.

It was midnight.

Recommended Reading About The Holidays:

POSITIVE MAGIC: *Occult Self-Help*
by Marion Weinstein, Phoenix Publishing Co., Custer, WA, 1978.

EARTH MAGIC: *A Dianic Book of Shadows*
by Marion Weinstein, Phoenix Publishing Co., Custer, WA, 1981.

THE GOLDEN BOUGH
by James George Frazer, MacMillan Paperbacks, Canada, Abridged Edition, 1969 and later printings.

WEST COUNTRY WICCA
by Rhiannon Ryall, Phoenix Publishing Co., Custer, WA, 1989.

THE WHEEL OF THE YEAR
by Pauline Campanelli, Llewellyn Publications, St. Paul, 1989.

THE WITCHES' ALMANAC
Prepared & Edited by Elizabeth Pepper & John Wilcock, Pentacle Press,Cambridge MA, 1991.

CIRCLE NETWORK NEWS (quarterly)
Selena Fox & Dennis Carpenter, Mt. Horeb, WI
P.O. Box 219, Mt. Horeb, WI 53572

About the author
Marion Weinstein divides her time between The Big City (New York) and her garden in Long Island, always surrounded by animals. She has been celebrating the ancient holidays for over twenty years.